CHA

JOURNEY

Robert Strand

New Leaf Press

First printing: April 1999

Cover by Janell Robertson

ISBN: 0-89221-470-8

Printed in the United States of America.

ENERGY FOR YOUR JOURNEY

Today . . . it's a topic of discussion when and where thinking people meet. Mankind, for the first time in history, is concerned about running out of energy. Efforts are being made to discover and tap into new and as of yet unused resources . . . solar, ocean tides, shale rock, and so on. And always, there is the ongoing search for perpetual energy of any kind. Energy must be renewable, abundant, and inexpensive.

Why then don't we realize that we already *have* an inexhaustible source of perpetual energy? It is an absolute necessity to have energy in order to achieve any kind of life success. The Bible says, *"God is the ENERGIZER within you!"* (Phil. 2:13; The Modern Language Bible).

WHAT IS YOUR LIFE MISSION?

An acquaintance who served as an officer in World War II told me that sentries were trained so that if an unidentified soldier or person suddenly appeared and could not state their identity and what their mission was about, they were to be shot without question. I have often wondered what would be the results if we today were confronted with such a policy?

State your life mission . . . or be shot!

Identity and mission are life and death issues! If we, you and I, as well as millions of others, know who we are and where we are going, think of the kinds of savings that could be achieved. It would save great gobs of time, mountains of money, stop the shedding of hot tears of regret, and take away the burden of heartaches for those we influence as well as ourselves. On the job, absenteeism would become obsolete, productivity of individuals and groups would soar, and no longer would we be putting up with meaninglessness of life from ourselves as well as our leaders.

With a mission statement in hand and heart . . . there would be the spine−tingling thrill that only comes from having achieved the seem− ingly impossible climb up the mountain. Tasks would be identified and completed! The purposes of life would be greater than simply to sur− vive! No more rootless kinds of living! Finding that mission and ful− filling that mission is the greatest, most vital life−activity you can do!

CHARTING YOUR JOURNEY

"Charting" and "journey" conjure up all kinds of mental pictures when I stop to do some thinking about both of these terms. Immediately I am struck with the thought of such names as Leif Ericson, Christopher Columbus, Marco Polo, Lewis and Clark, and Magellan. These were all explorers setting out on a journey of exploration. It sounds romantic . . . sailing into the unknown, finding and recording new worlds, uncovering new routes. Charting brings to mind a systematic plan . . . charts were consulted and created. Journey speaks of a trip, going someplace, experiencing new adventures, and meeting new people.

How about your life? We're about to sail into a new millennium! Have you even thought about charting where you plan to go, how you will get there, and what kind of a price you are willing to pay? The journey will be upon us before you know it. Think about it! It's not too late to begin to chart your course!

This is a wake-up call to action!

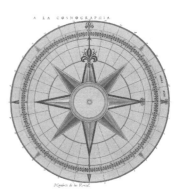

DO YOU HAVE A DREAM?

One of the most famous speeches of all time was delivered by Martin Luther King Jr. and is titled "I Have a Dream." It was a fabulous speech delivered with passion. Let me lift one quote from it: "I have a dream that one day every valley shall be exalted, every hill and mountain shall be made low, the rough places shall be made plain, and the crooked places shall be made straight, and the glory of the Lord will be revealed and all flesh shall see it together. This is our hope. . . . With this faith we will be able to hew out of the mountain of despair a stone of hope. With this faith we will be able to transform the jangling discords of our nation into a beautiful symphony of brotherhood."

Do you have a dream that drives you into this next century? Without a dream there is no hope! So dream a big dream on which you can build your future of hope!

LISTEN TO THE VOICES

Imagine that you have entered a family room. You have come late. When you arrived, others have preceded you and the discussion is going full blast. It's heated, in fact too heated for anyone among them to pause and bring you current or tell you what this is all about. You just don't jump in without listening for a while. You attempt to pick up the tenor of the argument . . . cautiously, maybe, you might put your oar into the water of debate. You make a statement, someone answers you, you answer them, somebody comes to your defense, another argues against you. And so it continues . . . you take part, then you must depart . . . with the discussion still vigorously in progress.

Listening to the voices of others might not necessarily mean only listening to internal voices. We are to listen and learn. What are the voices around you saying?

After all this input . . . the choices of life are still yours to make. That's where listening to that still small voice in the quiet of your soul makes sense. It's not that God always speaks in the thunder or lightning or with a loud clamoring voice. Often He can only be heard in the quiet . . . the still small voice is not intrusive and clamorous. For the journey, cultivate the art of listening before you take an action.

THE E.R.A. OF ACHIEVEMENT

There is a simple technique which has been most helpful to many people who have learned how to achieve meaningful objectives. Underline it, write it down, memorize it, and refer to it often!

It starts with you! You must *EXERCISE* your own personal power of choice — which only you can decide how and when to exercise. It's one of the most powerful forces in this world and it's yours to use.

The second step is to *REJECT* the negative thoughts which tend to plague too many of us. You always will have the negative to overcome. It might be voiced by others in loud or subtle ways. Or you may be sabotaging yourself from within.

And last, *ACCEPT* the positive, life-giving, and life-changing thought which you can uncover and discover from the greatest book on achievement ever written . . . the Bible, God's guidebook on living.

WHAT ABOUT THE Y2K ISSUE?

The year 2000 is almost upon us . . . so what? According to a recent Wells Fargo Bank/Gallup Poll, five million small businesses are at risk! Of these, 330,000 are projected to close. 370,000 will be severely crippled and on the brink of failure. Further, of the businesses surveyed, 75 percent have done nothing about it and 50 percent don't plan to.

What's all this furor about? It's not a complicated technical issue but it will take time to re-write programs, purchase new software, replace computers, correct the BIOS — all to correct an inherent error. Bright people who developed and programmed the early computers were concerned about every digit and attempted to save every bit of space. Presto, the Y2K issue! They simply wrote all dates with the last two digits. Thus, when the year 2000 rolls around . . . computers will indicate it as oo. No problem, except that it might be reading it as 1900 and send out bills to customers for overdue statements of 100 years of service. Yes, this is widespread and pervasive . . . but not a complex issue. Then, to complicate matters, the year 2000 is also leap year! (Interestingly, if we all had Apple computers, this would not be a problem at all because they've taken care of it long ago.)

Jesus Christ told an interesting story about people who built houses on the rock or on the sand. The storms of life beat upon both types . . . but the house built on the sand was destroyed. The silicone chip is the foundational building block of computers and it will continue on after the year 2000. All of this coming havoc brings to mind the question of the ages: Upon what are you building your life? Or better yet, upon whom are you building your life?

Yes, computers and technology are necessary to our modern day living — but the issues of life are much more important! The people who are building upon the sand are the people who have heard the life-giving words of Jesus and have failed to put them into practice. The rain will come down and the winds will blow. Will the Y2K time bomb explode your house with a great crash or will you survive because you have built your house on the ROCK?

WHO'S AFFECTED BY THE Y₂K BUG?

Another question is, "What's affected or what is anticipated to be affected?" The best minds are projecting that mainframe and personal computers will be, just for starters. Then consideration must be given to "process" control systems such as telephone switches, numeric control systems, electric generation control, and distribution systems. But it doesn't stop there . . . digital watches, VCRs, application software dealing with inventory or payroll, spreadsheets, operating systems, and the "BIOS!"

What is the "BIOS?" This is buried deep in the operating systems of all computers. Without the BIOS in proper working order you cannot even turn on a computer. How widespread is this problem? Ninety-three percent of all PCs built before 1997 have this problem,

47 percent of PCs built in 1997, and 20 percent of PCs built in 1998 have it!

Think of the impact this could have with the cost to detect and fix; the inconvenience and disruption . . . and always the liability issue. Some of the projected cost for General Motors is set at $350 to $500 million. Prudential Insurance is looking at $150 million. The estimated cost worldwide is somewhere between $300 and $600 BILLION! This will be a financial blood-bath! By comparison, the Los Angeles earthquake cost $60 BILLION, the Vietnam War cost $500 BIL-LION!

"It is written: 'Man does not live on *computers* alone, but on every word that comes from the mouth of God' " (Matt. 4:4; NIV, paraphrased).

Yes . . . do all you can to ward off the Y2K bug. Prepare and pay

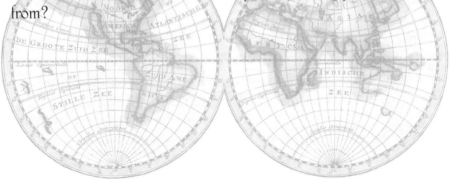

the price early! It is important that all systems continue to function when the new year of 2000 rolls around. But this is also to warn us that there are other issues of greater importance to you than whether your computers will function in the new millennium. How will you function in the new Mill? Where will you be drawing your life-source from?

LEARN HOW TO CELEBRATE!

Sam Walton devoted his life to the building of Wal–Mart stores into the nation's largest retailer. On April 5, 1992, he died after a long battle with cancer. Shortly following his death, more than 15,000 stockholders of Wal–Mart Stores, Inc. bid a fond farewell to Mr. Walton during a very emotional annual meeting in Fayetteville, Arkansas. This meeting was marked by hugs, tears, and sing–a–longs dedicated to the late Arkansas billionaire and what he had done for his investors.

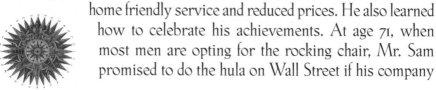

Walton created this most successful chain of stores through down–home friendly service and reduced prices. He also learned how to celebrate his achievements. At age 71, when most men are opting for the rocking chair, Mr. Sam promised to do the hula on Wall Street if his company could rack up a net pre-tax profit of more than 8 percent over the next reporting period. When Wal-Mart achieved this outstanding goal, Walton strapped on a grass skirt over his business suit and danced along with some traditional Hawaiian dancers and musicians on the sidewalk in front of a Wall Street office building!

This plain-living, unassuming, humble man who became a billionaire through entrepreneurship will be fondly remembered for his many business accomplishments. But those who knew him well will remember his youthful ability to celebrate his and others' successes!

What will they remember about you after you are gone?

LIFE IS A SPIRITUAL JOURNEY, TOO

The best that one can do in this life is to embark on that wonderful journey to the center where God is dwelling. No matter how you have started, you are to fight to continue on that journey no matter how many obstacles or problems or difficulties are thrown in your path. This journey has enemies, which no doubt you have discovered or will soon discover. Innately one knows this journey will be a battle. Also, one knows that in order to serve this transcendent God to the best of human ability, there must be a continually on-going alignment of this human self with the immanent God within, above, and everywhere omnipresent. One must always strive to realize and fulfill the blueprint of God with this finite human life. This is a journey to become the person God has created one to be!

NOTHING IS ORDINARY

The noted and accomplished English artist William Wolcott traveled to New York City in 1924 in order to record some of his artistic impressions of this extraordinary city.

One morning as he was visiting in the office of a former colleague the urge to sketch came over him. He immediately looked for some paper upon which to do the sketching. His eye fastened on paper lying on the desk of his friend and he asked, "May I have that?"

His friend replied, "That's just plain, ordinary wrapping paper."

Not wanting to lose the inspiration of the moment, Wolcott took the wrapping paper in hand and said, "Nothing is ordinary if you know how to use it."

And on that very ordinary wrapping paper Wolcott drew two

sketches. Later that year the first sold for $500 and the other $1,000! Quite staggering sums for 1924.

As you view your own life and that of your family . . . never forget that "NOTHING IS ORDINARY!"

CALCULATED RISK-TAKING

Too many people are not willing to take a risk because of the cost involved. Others might be willing to risk a bit of ridicule from others in their industry. And then there are the real risk-takers, people who are willing to risk all in even creating a whole new industry. Real risk-takers live by the philosophy of Samuel Johnson who said: *"Nothing will ever be attempted if all possible objections must first be overcome."*

A traveling salesman by the name of King Camp Gillette had problems finding a regular shave. He dreamed up a cockeyed invention that caused metallurgical engineers at M.I.T. to snicker. There was no way a piece of metal could be made razor sharp enough to provide a clean shave and yet cheap enough to be disposed of. Only 51 blades sold the first year, 90,844 were sold the

next year, and you know the rest is history.

Mary Kay Ash had the audacity to think that beauty products for women could be sold at home party shows. She believed skin care products could be sold in small groups of women looking for better ways to improve their image. Her first show produced only $1.50 in sales! She had risked her entire life savings on this venture. She went back and refined her sales techniques, revamped the packaging, and changed her attitude. She did $34,000 in home retail sales that first year. Within 15 years, Mary Kay had 150,000 consultants producing more than $200 million in gross sales and many of them are driving pink Cadillacs.

Charles House took an ultimate kind of risk. He was head of

corporate engineering at Hewlett-Packard and ignored an order from the co-founder to stop working on a high-quality, large screen video monitor. House pressed ahead and the monitor has been used for heart transplant operations as well as for space travel — 17,000 units were sold the first year rather than the projected 30. And HP bestowed on House a medal for "Extraordinary contempt and defiance beyond the normal call of engineering duty."

Anything worth achieving in life involves risk! Will Rogers said: *"You've got to go out on a limb sometimes, because that's where the fruit is."*

THE YEAR 2000 ... WHAT TO DO?

Just think — when the new millennium rolls around, it will be the turning of the clock to introduce a new century, a new millennium, and a leap year all rolled into one huge event. How many generations of people have had this privilege? The excitement is building, as well as the warnings of dire doom and gloom. What should we be doing in preparation? Perhaps the following suggestions will jolt you into action:

- Wake up before it's too late!
- Identify any high-risk areas in your lifestyle!
- Have a strategy in place and have a contingency plan made, too!
- Consider all of your options — should you simply fix or replace?

- Check out your insurance!
- Your "due diligence" will be critical!
- Make sure you and your family are all on the same page, relationally!
- Is your spiritual life solid and committed? Will it stand the test of any possible coming storm?

SPHÆRA ARMILLARIS

WHAT'S ALL THIS FUSS ABOUT ANYWAY?

By now just about everyone's heard of the upcoming millennium and the computer bug along with it. But are you aware that the year 2000 may not be 2000 after all? Calendars are relative things which measure the passing of time. They are man-made and are not absolute!

There's no universal reason that the year 2000 will be that. For the Chinese it will be the year 4698. For the Jews it will be the year 5761. For the Muslims, whose calendar is based on the cycles of the moon, the year A.D. 2000 will be the year 1420!

Our present calendar-keeping comes to us from the Romans who got it from the Egyptians. Think about this . . . when Julius Caesar stole the Egyptian way of figuring the years, he added 90 extra days to the year 46 B.C. because the astronomer Sosigenes said it would con-form better to the seasons of the year.

But there's more. This Julian calendar was modified in 1582 by Pope Gregory who wiped out ten days because by that time spring was arriving on March 11 instead of March 21, the date that had been set in the 4th century. Now really, folks, what is all the fuss about? If Pope Gregory and Julius Caesar can do away with days and weeks, surely we in this new millennium are sophisticated enough to take care of these mistaken two digits without any more fussing. Right?! Sure. Besides, is there really such a thing as the year 2000?

So . . . who really is keeping track of time, correct time, real time, exact time, in this universe?

The Bible tells us that *"There is a time for everything, and a season for every activity under heaven"* (Eccles. 3:1). If you were to read on a bit further in this same chapter you will discover that God *"has made everything beautiful in its time. He has also set eternity in the hearts of men; yet they cannot fathom what God has done from beginning to end"* (Eccles. 3:11).

Jesus asked the question: *"How is it that you don't know how to interpret this present time?"* (Luke 12:56). There is only One keeper of the real time! It is imperative that we keep in step with eternity, for the day is coming when all of man's best efforts to mark out calendars will be over and done. Then what will be important? Your relation-ship and my relationship with the Creator of the universe!

THREE WAYS TO
RUIN YOUR LIFE

Billy Graham was the speaker at the funeral service of Dawson Trotman, the founder of "The Navigators." Some of his remarks were remembered by Leroy Eims to include:

"There are three ways to destroy one's life:

1. Give in to the slothful nature and do nothing. These folks just lie around and fry in their own fat.

2. Give one's self to a particular goal, work hard toward that goal, and upon attaining the goal find that it was not of great value. Many have found only bitterness and tears at this conclusion.

3. Dabble. Accomplish many little things, but nothing of any "import."

Graham's conclusion was that Dawson's life exhibited none of these self-defeating characteristics.

Now, what about your life? It is time to take an inventory! Perhaps it's time to re-chart your life course, set some different goals, and dedicate your remaining years to something bigger than your present lifestyle.

ARE YOU FOR REAL?

On February 12, 1998, Chan Gailey was named as the new head coach of the Dallas Cowboys. It caught the football world by surprise, to say the least. What was interesting was the spin the media was putting on this selection. Gailey had coached Troy State to a Division II national championship, Samford U. to a dismal 5 and 6 record, the Birmingham Fire as part of the defunct World Football league, and most recently was offensive coordinator of the Pittsburgh Steelers.

In Birmingham, Alabama, Paul Finebaum, local radio sports talk host, interviewed Richard Scott, sportswriter for the *Birmingham Post Herald*. Scott was a long-time friend and admirer of Gailey.

Finebaum probed Gailey's past and Scott did a credible job in defending Gailey's intelligence, organizational skills, coaching ability, and people skills. Most interesting was that Gailey's spirituality was mentioned in sharp contrast to former Cowboy coaches Jimmy Johnson and Barry Switzer. Finebaum then asked, "Is Gailey for real?"

Richard Scott responded, "Chan Gailey is the finest Christian man I have ever known. His impact on me is so great that I can say that other than Jesus Christ himself, no man has had a greater impact on my decision to become a Christian than Chan Gailey. Chan Gailey is the reason I made a decision to become a Christian. I saw what he had in his life that I did not have in mine, and I wanted to have it too." (Loosely taken from a WERC AM 960 talk show in Birmingham.)

Did you catch the impact of these words? "No man has had a greater impact on my decision to become a Christian than Chan Gailey." What do the people who come in contact with you say about your Christian witness and lifestyle? What a tribute! This is how I want to be remembered! How about you?

ON MISSING THE MONA LISA

Rabbi Mordecai E. Zeitz tells about the painting of the Mona Lisa which was stolen from the Louvre in Paris in 1911. The painting was missing for more than two years. What was so incredible about this disappearance is that more people came to see the empty spot where the painting had hung than had ever come to see it in the previous 12 years.

Do you, like me, find this to be an intriguing bit of information or at least an interesting commentary about life? It seems to point to an all-too-human tendency to fail to appreciate our precious things while we have them. We don't appreciate what we have until it's gone. Then . . . we are painfully aware of these blank spaces. Further . . . our full attention is then riveted on what has come up missing. Blessings and precious things that we always seem to have are easily overlooked until they are gone. Good health is taken for granted until it's gone . . . a best friend is understood to always be there . . . a marriage that started out right but is neglected can end with void and hurt. That which we always seem to have is too easily taken for granted.

The songwriter penned it correctly: *"Count your blessings; name them one by one."* May all our days be lived out in appreciation for what is precious in living.

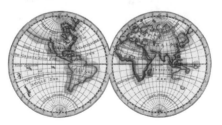

CONVICTIONS OR PREFERENCES?

The Random House dictionary defines "conviction" as "the state of being convinced; a fixed belief." It is simply the positive belief that some things are right and some things are wrong. A "preference" is defined as "that which is preferred or chosen." A conviction and a preference are not the same things. Convictions are strong beliefs and do not change easily. Preferences are fickle and can often change.

Just about every day of living you are confronted with questions and decisions. For example . . . when faced with a dilemma, do I do what is right in order to please God or shall I forget about convictions and do what is wrong so that I will please others? Knowing what the truth is, is almost a universal thing among us but living it out is much more rare.

One of the major changes we are experiencing as a society today is that no longer is the knowledge of truth universal. Today, truth has been set aside for political correctness and feel-good philosophies. We are urged to tone down our convictions so that no one will be offended. We have become so agreeable that no longer can we be the salt and light in a dark world. We are losing the distinctive of black and white, right and wrong, in a blurring of lines and new definitions.

Solomon, the wisest man who ever lived, observed that the *"Fear of man will prove to be a snare, but whoever trusts in the Lord is kept safe"* (Prov. 29:25). What will you live by? Convictions or preferences?

CAN YOU BE CONTENT?

One Sunday morning I was part of a congregation in Branson, Missouri, that was being ministered to by a humble, contented vocalist and guitar player. We were all touched by his story and his musical ministry. In fact, many in the audience sat with tears running down their cheeks. What's so special about that?

Tony Melendez was born without arms. He was a thalidomide baby. No arms and a left clubfoot . . . yet, with his feet and toes, played the guitar beautifully! We sat enraptured, each of us with two good arms and hands, as he shared his story. It was one of the most moving and touching meetings I have ever been a part of. He told of his struggle to exist, to learn how to do things with two feet, driving with no arms and hands in a specially built car, getting married, adopting two kids, and making a life of ministry that blessed others.

Tony spoke of the difficulties that had been his. But then he began talking about the contentment of his life. How God had been good to him in sparing his life, giving him a life, talent to use, and a family who loved. We were all chastised . . . how did we get up that morning? Complaining about another day? Unhappy with health, spouse, job, family, car, house, or weather?

As we all walked out into the sunshine, my thought was: *I have so much with which to be content, why complain ever again?*

Tony, like Paul the Apostle, had learned this secret to living a fulfilling life: *"For I have learned to be content whatever the circum-stances"* (Phil. 4:11). Even the bad things and the bad times can be an occasion to experience the goodness of God — especially if we are to learn how to be content.

WHY WORRY ABOUT THE FUTURE?

Question: Do you worry? Lots of Americans worry and these same people take more medications to forget about these worries than any other nation in world history!

Worry is nothing more or less than paying interest on trouble before it comes. Worry is one of the greatest obstacles to success in living. When you worry it's like sitting in a rocking chair . . . lots of motion but no progress. Leo Buscaglia wrote: "Worry never robs tomorrow of its sorrow, it only saps today of its joy."

Studies have been made about the things that worry people. About 40 percent of our worries never happen, approximately 30 percent has already happened, 12 percent are over unfounded health concerns, 10 percent involves the little daily insignificant worries that accomplish nothing. Add these all up and you realize that 92 percent of the time we worry for no good reason. That leaves only 8 percent of our worries that we can legitimately justify. Dr. Charles Mayo said, "Worry affects the circulation and the whole nervous system. I've never known a man who died from overwork, but I've known many who have died from doubt." In other words . . . worry can kill!

There really is only one simple solution to the worry problem: Don't worry about the things you cannot change. If you don't like your situation, don't worry, do something constructive about it! Less worry and more action will take care of most of your worry.

LEARN TO LISTEN

Professional golfer Tommy Bolt had established quite a reputation for himself with his temper. He threw clubs, he broke clubs, and he had temper tantrums. In one tournament, he was assigned a caddie whose reputation was that he talked constantly. Mr. Bolt told him to be quiet and completely discipline himself to only say, "Yes, Mr. Bolt" or "No, Mr. Bolt."

One of his tee shots dropped close to a tree. To reach the green he had to hit the ball under an overhanging branch and over water. He looked his shot over and considered his options. He was half talking to himself and halfway to his caddie, and asked, "Should I hit it with my five iron?"

The caddie having been duly warned, said, "No, Mr. Bolt."

Bolt's temper erupted and he replied, "What do you mean, not a five iron? Just watch this shot!"

The caddie still following instructions, again said, "No, Mr. Bolt!" But Bolt didn't listen . . . he carefully lined up the shot and hit it to the green and it stopped a couple of feet from the hole, a great recovery stroke.

Satisfied with himself, Bolt handed the club to the caddie and remarked, "What do you think about that? And it's okay for you to talk, now."

The caddie said, "Mr. Bolt, that wasn't your ball." That little mistake cost Tommy Bolt a two-shot penalty and lots of prize money.

The message is quite simple: Learn to listen to others and be nice. It's amazing what you can learn to help you along life's journey.

DON'T FORGET TO HAVE FUN ON THE JOURNEY

This book is not about increasing your bottom line but about maximizing the journey, increasing the enjoyment, succeeding in living, adding to your store of wisdom, and working smarter. Mix these elements with joy and your journey can be fun.

At some point, you will likely be looking back on the life you have lived . . . maybe in your advanced years or even from the perspective of your deathbed. I'm speculating, but I doubt that you will be thinking about how much money you have made or the possessions you have collected. Rather, I believe you will be musing about a life that has been fulfilling, relationships that have been made and kept, the loving quality of your lifestyle, what you have given to others, and how enjoyable the journey has been. There can be plenty of regrets if you have forgotten to have fun along the way.

Having attained some or all of your goals will be wonderful! It will be great to have achieved financial security, to have been a responsible family person, to have used the God—given gifts to their fullest, and to have helped others along the way.

When you come to the end of your life . . . what really counts are your relationships — the people you will be seeing in heaven and the anticipation of an eternity spent with the Creator of life. A life lived without joy is an empty one. The challenge of Paul the Apostle is to learn how to *"rejoice in the Lord!"*

STRESS . . . TOO MUCH OR TOO LITTLE?

Stress can be good or bad! In the root definition it's a physics term, an engineering term, according to Random House Dictionary, "the action on a body of any system of balanced forces whereby strain or deformation results." Too much stress on the human body can deform it through the loss of sleep, high blood pressure, irritability, and more. Too little stress and there is no achievement.

Without stress on the strings you could get no music out of a guitar, piano, or violin. But too much and there is a breakdown. How we learn to cope with stress in our living will largely affect our lifestyle and achievement levels. The key word from our definition would be "balance."

Perhaps you need to identify the source of stress in your life.

Could it be that added stress has come out of disagreement with family members or a fellow worker or a load of guilt you may be harboring? If it's a people problem you can talk it out, apologize, or make it right. A second method is to find some way in which to release the pressure. You cannot live with clenched fists all the time. Take time away, read a good book, take a walk, go on a vacation, shift your scenery, do something nice for someone you love.

SPHÆRA ARMILLARIS

These two simple little steps can go a long way toward balancing the load of stress in your life.

TEN RULES FOR LIVING IN THE NEW MILLENNIUM

Some things are eternal no matter what millennium you find them in. Our present culture has placed great emphasis on being able to do your own thing, look out for number one, be a rugged individualist. But a standard has been raised which had never been equaled by any other document of truth. It is the foundation upon which previous civilizations have been built. These truths have stood the test of time and eternal authorship.

Today, too many of us are bothered because these truths have been stated in the negative — THOU SHALT NOT! We would rather have them stated in the positive. But consider how long and laborious they would become. God could have said, "Adam and Eve, you must eat of every fruit-bearing tree in this garden beginning in the northeast corner and proceeding to the southwest corner. Do not overlook or ignore any growing thing. It is yours for life and nourishment. However there is a single tree, in the middle of this garden from which you must not eat, etc., etc."

It was so much more simple to state: *"You are free to eat from any tree in the garden; but you must not eat from the tree of knowledge."*

Yes, I know that these commands are familiar to you . . . but how about re-reading them again. They will be foundational for the 21st century as well as for the entire 1,000 years of the new millennium.

1. You shall have no other gods before me.
2. You shall not make for yourself an idol.
3. You shall not misuse the name of the Lord your God.

4. Remember the Sabbath day by keeping it holy.
5. Honor your father and your mother.
6. You shall not murder.
7. You shall not commit adultery.
8. You shall not steal.
9. You shall not give false testimony.
10. You shall not covet.

No misunderstandings, no difficult language, nothing obtuse . . . simple, to-the-point guidelines until we are ushered into eternity! Commandments — not suggestions — by which to live!

HELPING OTHERS ALONG THE JOURNEY

Zig Ziglar writes, "I've built my life and my business on a concept, namely that you can have everything in life you want if you will just help enough other people get what they want."

Sam Walton expressed much the same life philosophy, but said it this way, "I quickly learned that when I enriched others, I also enriched myself."

Perhaps you can recall from your scouting days that part of the Scout teaching was to do at least one good deed every day. One of the most intriguing concepts of life is that when you do something good for others . . . some way, somehow, someday there will be a significant return. This is one of the major laws of sowing and reaping inherent in this world originally planned by the Creator. And there is also a scientific answer to this doing for others. When you do the good deed or the kind action, your brain is flooded with "serotonin" which has been called the "feel-good" neurotransmitter that is so important for energizing us.

The Bible put it like this: "*Do not be deceived: God cannot be mocked. A man reaps what he sows.*" Now pay special attention to this next part as it's expressed in a negative and a positive sense. "*The one who sows to please his sinful nature, from that nature will reap destruction; the one who sows to please the Spirit will reap eternal life. **Let us not become weary in doing good, for at the proper time we will reap a harvest if we do not give up! THEREFORE, as we have opportunity, let us do good to all people!***" (Gal. 6:7–10; NIV).

To give yourself a serotonin lift today . . . do something special for someone who cannot repay you in kind!

JUST SAY "THANKS!"

Jack Nicklaus, one of the most legendary golfers, is also legendary for expressing thanks. This gesture of expressing thanks began for Jack in the very early days of his career when he was too poor to stay in luxury hotels and he stayed with people in their homes. Always he would write a special note of thanks expressing gratefulness for their show of hospitality. To this day, many of these people prize the notes he wrote to them. Then times and the fortunes of golf changed for him . . . he became a superstar in golf and business and he could afford to stay anywhere he chose. But that didn't change his habit of expressing thanks. He still goes through life looking for ways in which to express his gratitude to others who have been of help.

Jesus Christ set the example for all of us to follow. As you read of

Him through the Gospels you note that He always gave thanks before He ate, expressed thanks to the Heavenly Father, and showed appreciation for any demonstration of love given to him. One example is His thanks to the woman who anointed His head with expensive oil and who washed His feet with her tears. Gratitude!

In life, in living, in business, in personal relationships, you just can't say "thank you" too often. Do as Jack and Jesus do and did . . . say it often, say it to all who need it, say it to those you love, say it to those who have been a help!

THANK YOU . . . for being a reader of this book!

GETTING AWAY

Jesus Christ lived with a philosophy that could be expressed like this: Come apart before you come a part. No one ever lived with as much to do in such a short period of time while on this earth. In fact, He sandwiched into three years accomplishments that have blessed all of mankind. Yet, He still took plenty of time away.

Once more, He is the supreme example on how to live productively while on this earth. You may be thinking that "it's better to burn out than to rust out." But I would argue that a well-rested person could be far more productive than a harried, tired, never-on-vacation type of person. Learn to take real vacations, ones in which you are truly away.

Peter Lynch was an amazing financial wizard who earned Fidelity tens of millions of dollars through his stock picks. It was he who made the Magellan Mutual Fund one of the largest and most successful in mutual fund history. But he walked away from it all . . . another victim of too-early burnout. Perhaps if the top executives who were taking their vacations had also insisted on Peter taking his, he could still be making those amazing picks. Much can be lost when we ignore the body's need to rest.

Jesus placed a very high value on time away, time alone for meditation, thinking, praying, and re-charging the mind and body. If you are going to make it for the long journey, you, too, should be getting away from it all before it's too late.

DON'T SWEAT THE SMALL STUFF

Richard Carlson, Ph.D., has written a best-selling book, *Don't Sweat The Small Stuff,* in which he says this decision to not sweat it lies at the heart of a high-quality of life. It's a way of keeping life in true perspective.

Now, let's think about his premise for a moment. Life is crammed and jammed full of things. Every day brings decisions that are important and things that need to be dealt with — demands are everywhere and it's so easy to become embroiled in the day-to-day, moment-by-moment-ness of it all. If you can become one of those special people who refuse to sweat the small stuff you have built a bumper for yourself in this life. You can then save lots of energy which is frittered away and focus it on the big things . . . creativity, problem-solving, building lasting relationships, and creating abundance.

How you relate to the small stuff is directly tied to how effectively you can deal with it. I'm not telling you to ignore this small stuff . . . but to put it into proper relationship with the big picture.

Life may not be perfect and if you think it could be, I've got news for you — it will never be perfect because none of us have arrived. But in doing this little exercise of discipline you can enhance the quality of life and improve your chances for experiencing more success.

Instead of the little stuff, look at the big picture! Life is wonderful! Think of all the things that need to be treasured! Dream big dreams! Revel in relationships! All become more of a reality when you have learned how to not sweat the small stuff!

ELEMENTS OF A GOOD MISSION STATEMENT

Do you have a mission statement that you live by? Perhaps the company you work for has one . . . but a personal one? Sure, why not? Think of some of the world's great leaders and their mission easily comes to mind. Abraham Lincoln's mission was to save the Union of our nation. Franklin Delano Roosevelt's mission was to lead this Union through the Great Depression. Mother Teresa's mission was to show compassion to the untouchables in their dying moments of life. Nehemiah's mission was to rebuild the broken-down walls of Jerusalem. John the Baptist's mission was to prepare the way for Jesus Christ, the Lamb of God. Jesus Christ's mission is to seek and to save all who are lost! What is your mission statement?

A good statement of mission should encompass these three clear elements:

1. It should be no more than a sentence in length.
2. It should be so easily understood that 12 year olds can grasp the meaning.
3. You should be able to recite it at all times, even under great stress.

Once this statement has been created, adhering to it will save you from getting tangled up with details that become obstacles on your journey!

BE A FRUIT
INSPECTOR

Over the years I have been richly blessed by some friends I have made and, unfortunately, I have also been ripped off by some I thought were friends. I have been helped and rewarded by people I have hired to be employees and have been hurt by many failures I have also hired. My record is not stellar, even after using all kinds of background checks or evaluation tools.

Even Jesus Christ was hurt by people whom he had chosen to be part of his inner circle of followers. He chose 12 and one of them betrayed him. But Jesus also has given us some guidelines for those of us who must hire or select people in our world.

He tells us that *"by their fruit you will recognize them . . . every good tree bears good fruit and a bad tree bears bad fruit"* (Matt. 7:16–17). Yes, this seems obvious, but it's a truth which can be lost in the process.

When you are cultivating a new friendship, when you are voting, when you are hiring, when you are evaluating, please take a good long and hard look at the results of the person under consideration. Check out what this person has produced — good or bad fruit. And always, follow the advice of the wisest man who ever lived on this earth, Jesus Christ who told us to . . . BE A FRUIT INSPECTOR!

BECOME A SERVANT

The way up is the way down! The way to succeed is to put others first! To reach the top is to start at the bottom! To really live is to learn how to die! However, many who are attempting to climb the ladder of success do not believe these concepts work. They relegate these principles to another day long past, something for another time.

Today's conventional wisdom is that for you to be a number one, you must first and foremost take care of number one.

The reality? The surest road to success for all of us is to put employees, customers, friends, and family first.

Who says this is the way to experiencing true success? Simply the world's greatest authority on success and how relationships really work. Jesus said, "*The greatest among you will be your servant. For whoever exalts himself will be humbled and whoever humbles himself will be exalted"* (Matt. 23:11–12).

Why are we unwilling to learn from either Jesus Christ or from other contemporary examples of people who have put this concept to work? Nowhere did I say that this is the easy way to success — I'm saying it is the surest way to success. Yes, it's costly, but it always works! Learn how to become a servant so that the journey becomes one of success!

THIS WORLD NEEDS LEADERS . . .

Who use their influence at the right times for the right reasons;

Who take a greater share of the blame and a much smaller
share of the credit;

Who lead themselves successfully before attempting to lead
others;

Who continue to search for the best answer and will not settle
for the familiar one;

Who add value to the people they lead;

Who work for the benefit of others and not only for personal
gain;

Who handle themselves with their heads and handle others with
their hearts;

Who know the way . . . go the way . . . and show the way;

Who inspire and motivate rather than intimidate and manipulate;

Who live with people to know their problems and live with God in order to solve them;

Who realize that their dispositions are more important than their positions;

Who mold opinions instead of allowing opinion polls;

Who understand that an institution is a reflection of their own character;

Who never place themselves above others except in carrying responsibilities;

Who will be as honest in small things as in great things;

Who discipline themselves so they will not be disciplined by others;

Who encounter setbacks and turn them into comebacks;

Who follow a moral compass that points in the right direction regardless of the trends!

THIS WORLD DESPERATELY NEEDS THIS KIND OF LEADERS — PEOPLE WHO STILL BELIEVE THAT CHARACTER COUNTS, WHO DISCIPLINE THEMSELVES TO DEVELOP LEADERSHIP CHARACTER! How about *YOU* stepping up to be counted among them?!

SABOTAGING OUR OWN JOURNEY

While you were young, it may have been well-meaning parents and teachers who sabotaged your success. But being good students, it didn't take any of us too long before we learned how to do it to ourselves! We all do a job on ourselves some of the time — but some among us have turned it into an art.

There are some patterns of thinking that self-sabotaging people have used to get in the way of any success. It's an inside kind of job. It's a way of orchestrating failure. What are some of the ways?

BLAMING OTHERS: It's the first step downward. It's so insidious because on the surface it may seem to be an excellent excuse. "How can you expect me to be a success at _____ (you fill in the blank) when _____ (he, she, my mother, my father, my boss, my job, lack of money, poor opportunities, etc., take your pick) is standing in my way?"

Okay, see how easy that is? And when you do it you give control of your life over to someone or something else.

SETTING IMPOSSIBLE GOALS: This is sneaky but it looks like you are getting lots of things done. What do I mean? EXAMPLE: Suppose this person has been an entry-level wage earner for the past ten years and decides the rut is too much. So this person resolves to lose weight, start an exercise program, upgrade computer skills, and go to college to get an MBA.

These are all good possible goals. But each one of them in itself is a challenge, let alone attempting all at once. If you could hear this person tell you all these goals it sounds great . . . but down deep, does this person want to fail so they could still be uncomfortable where they are?

SETTING AN IMPOSSIBLE TIME SCHEDULE: No matter how enthused, how well meaning, how intent on success . . . there is one factor you cannot escape — to do these things takes time!

It's sort of like the idealistic, naive young man who climbs the mountain to visit the resident guru. When he gets there he says, "I want spiritual enlightenment and I want it now!"

NOT DOING WHAT MUST BE DONE: If you happen to be like most people, one of the hardest things to accept is that you might be acting out this kind of lifestyle. To lose weight, you must change eating habits. To save for retirement, you must set it aside each paycheck.

No matter what you want in life, no matter where you are headed, you must always start from the same place. You start from where you are right now.

FAITH FOR THE JOURNEY

When you have come to the end of your rope,
    When you have exhausted all the answers
        you have learned,
When you have come to the
    Edge of all the light you know,

And are about to step off into
    The darkness of the unknown,

Faith is knowing one of two things will happen:
    There will be something solid to stand on,
            Or
You will learn how to fly!

A PERSONAL CREED TO LIVE BY

What do you believe? What do you live by? What is there in your life that is the moral compass from which direction can be found? I don't know about you, but . . .

I believe that imagination can be stronger than knowledge.
>   That myth has a life of its own and is more potent than history.

I believe that dreams and hopes are more powerful motivators than are facts.
>   That hope will always triumph over experience.
>   That love and laughter are the cures for grief.
>   That people who know their God will ultimately triumph.
>   That character is important in all that you do.

I believe that the sun will ultimately rise again tomorrow.

That no matter what you have done you can start over again.

I believe that the three most powerful elements in life are faith, hope, and love.

That God is still alive today.

That God is still in control.

That the world belongs to people of faith.

That people with hope can overcome any life obstacle.

That the greatest of these is love.

That love is stronger than is death!

INTEGRITY IS STILL IMPORTANT

It's a simple concept, but oh so powerful in your journey: *"In order to succeed at anything you must keep your word!"* What is "integrity"? It simply means to be honest when nobody is looking. It is a total agreement between what you do and what you say. It is derived from a root word that means "whole, entire, undiminished" — what appears to be and what is reality are the same.

The power of integrity is awesome! Think — how would it change this world if all national leaders were completely honest? How would your life be affected today if all the politicians who promised to cut your taxes, had? How would your life be changed today if you had kept all the promises you had made? This kind of thinking boggles the mind.

Perhaps most important of all are the promises you have made to yourself. Who is it that said, "To thine own self be true"? When you are disciplined enough to keep your own word to yourself, some very amazing things happen. Think of all the nagging that would end.

What would the benefits be if you kept your word in all of your relationships? This carries with it a boomerang effect. When you keep your word, people will perceptibly change the way they talk about you and the way in which you are perceived. When integrity has been proven, you will be given more and greater responsibilities. You have opportunities to move on up to higher levels of achievement. Why? Because this is one of the surest and most guaranteed avenues to true success in life. Why? Because this concept works!

The man who exemplified truth more than any other said: *"Well done, good and faithful servant! You have been faithful with a few things; I will put you in charge of many things. Come and share your master's happiness!"* (Matt. 25:21; NIV).

ELEMENTS OF A SUCCESSFUL JOURNEY

No matter what you have been told or have believed, you *don't* necessarily need money, education, connections, position, or good health to succeed. In every nation, every period of history, in good times and bad, there have been people who have succeeded without any of these things! If you think you can't make it without these — re-think it!

The Gallups took a poll and wrote a book, *The Great American Success Story.* The polling question went something like this: What are the characteristics of successful people? Following are the answers in order of frequency:

1. Common sense
2. Special knowledge
3. Self-reliance

4. General intelligence
5. Ability to get things done
6. Leadership
7. Knowing right from wrong
8. Creativity and inventiveness
9. Self-confidence
10. Oral expression
11. Concern for others

Think about these things. Does anything strike you? Most of these characteristics you were born with! In other words, some of the most successful people in the world say that you started out in life with most of what you need in order to succeed. And what you haven't been born with, you can develop with discipline. Probably the biggest secret of success is that there are no special, inside secrets!